Presented to

_____

On the occasion of

_____

From

_____

Date

_____

Fast food for the Married Soul

Oscar & Crystal Jones

Fast food for the Married Soul

Oscar & Crystal Jones

Destiny House Publishing, LLC

Detroit, MI

Fast Food for the Married Soul

Published by Destiny House Publishing, LLC

Copyright ©2013 Oscar & Crystal Jones

ISBN-13: 978-1936867646

Unless otherwise stated, all scripture quotations are from the Holy Bible, King James Version. Scripture references that do not have the Bible version noted are the author's paraphrase.

Cover design and Publication Layout: Destiny House Publishing, LLC

Artwork from Dreamstime

Editing: Destiny House Publishing, LLC

ALL RIGHTS RESERVED

All rights reserved under International Copyright law. No part of this book may be reproduced or transmitted in any form or by any means: electronic, mechanical, including photocopying and recording, or by any information storage and retrieval system, without permission in writing from the publisher. Printed in the United States of America

For information:

Destiny House Publishing, LLC

www.destinyhousepublishing.com

email: inquiry@destinyhousepublishing.com

P.O. Box 19774 Detroit, MI 48219 888-890-9455

Table Of Contents

ADULTERY 1

AFFIRMATION 3

ANGER 7

CHILDREN AND STEPCHILDREN 9

COMMITMENT 13

COMMUNICATION 17

DATE NIGHT 21

DIVORCE 23

FORGIVENESS 27

GOD-CENTERED 29

HONESTY 31

HONOR 33

IN-LAWS 35

LOVE	39
LOYALTY	41
MONEY	43
ONENESS	47
SELFISHNESS	49
SEX	51
SUBMISSION	53
TRUST	57
WISDOM FOR WIVES	61
WISDOM FOR HUSBANDS	65
BUILDING A HEALTHY RELATIONSHIP	69
HOPE FOR HURTING MARRIAGES	73

HOW TO USE THIS BOOK

This book was created for marriages of all ages. It contains truths and short quotes to help strengthen and encourage marriages.

It is divided up into categories. Those categories are listed in alphabetical order. This allows the couple to go directly to the error of struggle and get quick help for their relationship. It's like marriage ministry express or marriage wisdom at a glance.

There are bonus sections at the back of the book: Wisdom Bites for the Whole Marriage

Wisdom for Husbands

Wisdom for Wives

Building A Healthy Marriage

and Hope for Hurting Marriages.

ADULTERY

> *Marriage is honourable in all, and the bed undefiled. For fornicators and adulterers God will judge.* Hebrews 13:4 KJV

Engaging in pornography, sexting, sexual imaginations, etc. IS adultery.

Adultery is senseless. Your actions cause so much hurt, it inflicts devastating damage on your marriage, it assaults the heart of your wife, children and others in relationship with you, it causes public humiliation, family and friends lose respect for you, you disconnect with the God of your salvation, and so on... Don't fall for the trap of the enemy.

Pornography devastates marriages. If you are caught up, seek God for deliverance and healing before it's too late.

Destroy adultery, pornography, sexting, chat rooms, lust, etc, before they destroy your marriage.

The Greener Grass Syndrome is a mirage. No one gets green grass without water and fertilizer.

Flirting is not innocent or harmless. It is selfish, inconsiderate, hurtful, and downright dangerous. Love the one you gave your promise to.

Maintaining a "friendship" with your ex is a setup for failure in your marriage.

Pay attention and make the necessary adjustments when your spouse warns you that someone is attracted to you.

Saying "I Do" doesn't deliver you from the spirit of lust. If you committed fornication before I do, it will be adultery after I do. Be wise enough to kill the lust in your own flesh so that it doesn't damage your relationship.

Dress in a way that honors your spouse. Save the revealing clothing for your bedroom.

If you are emotionally connected to another person you have cheated your spouse out of this part of you that you have chosen to invest in another.

Thinking about someone else while you are being sexually intimate with your spouse is adultery.

Pornography always seeks to draw your affection away from your spouse.

AFFIRMATION

> But exhort one another daily, while it is called Today; lest any of you be hardened through the deceitfulness of sin. Hebrews 3:13 KJV

To make your spouse feel affirmed, praise your spouse both privately and publicly.

Be your spouse's BIGGEST cheerleader.

Surprise your spouse with something off his/her "favorite" list.

Show appreciation to your spouse for actions you like. Don't just complain about the things you don't like.

Make your spouse remember why she/he said, I do.

Text or inbox your spouse, put a love note in his/her lunch or briefcase.

Take a genuine interest in your spouse's work and hobbies.

Celebrate each other's victories.

Affection and appreciative words give life to a dry marriage.

When your spouse does something positive, share it with your friends and family.

Reassuring your spouse daily helps them to be secure in the relationship.

Compliment your spouse in bed. It makes your physical relationship that much better.

Don't make your spouse feel inferior. You are not better than the person you married. You chose them just as they chose you.

Lovingly touch your spouse . It's affirmation without words.

You were born to be a blessing to your spouse.

Talking negatively about your spouse's weight is self-defeating. Only when your spouse feels good about themselves will you yield the best result.

Distance in a relationship comes due to a lack of attention.

Giving time to your spouse enhances your marriage.

There is always something for which you can affirm your spouse. Look for it.

ANGER

> *Refrain from anger and turn from wrath;*
> *do not fret—it leads only to evil.*
> *Psalms 37:8 NIV*

Don't let the sun go down on your anger. Stay up and talk it out.

When you and spouse do not agree, make sure you are attacking the issue and NOT each other.

Fight the enemy, not each other.

Be careful not to take your frustrations out on your spouse. Talk it out.

Smart couples choose their battles wisely. They do not fight over every irritation.

When you dig your heels in the sand, you get stuck. Let's work at reaching a solution to move forward.

Biting your tongue may be temporarily painful, but it saves your marriage from lasting devastation.

If one of you wins an argument, the marriage loses.

Anger never heals a marriage. In order to move forward in your marriage, you will have to let go of your anger.

Don't allow a problem in your marriage to become greater than the person you promised to love.

Choose your battles wisely. All battles are NOT meant to be fought.

Don't stew in your anger towards your spouse. You may find yourself in trouble with God. The wrath of man does not work the righteous of God. James 1:20

Anger puts your relationship at risk.

Your spouse is not your enemy, Satan is. Keep this truth in mind.

Caution: Losing your temper could cause you to lose your marriage.

Don't stew over an issue for longer than an hour. Deal with it and move on.

Touch to diffuse the situation. Agree in prayer. Set aside the emotion and deal with the problem.

Keep focus: The most important thing is to keep covenant.

CHILDREN AND STEPCHILDREN

> *Children are a heritage from the LORD, offspring a reward from him. Like arrows in the hands of a warrior are children born in one's youth. Blessed is the man whose quiver is full of them. They will not be put to shame when they contend with their opponents in court. Psalm 127:3-5 NIV*

Do not love your step-children any less than your biological children. Love them as if you gave birth to them.

Blended families can work. But we must put the work in.

His children and her children need to become our children.

Strong parenting skills undergird and encourage a strong marriage.

Train your children to respect your marriage and they will grow up to respect their own.

Don't allow your spouse to operate as a single parent. Two are better than one. It's the way God intended.

Don't undermine your spouse's authority/discipline with the children. Parent from the same page.

One day your children will be grown and gone. Keep your priorities straight in your marriage. Your spouse comes first.

Parents hand their children a script on how to conduct themselves in marriage. Children who are raised by harsh, spoiled, lustful, manipulative, abusive, disconnected, and/or unsubmissive parents will drag these same bad traits into their own marriages.

Be the type of spouse that you would want your child to marry. Because they are watching you.

It is unwise to disallow discipline from a stepparent.

Intentionally go after your spouse's children. Love your way into their hearts.

Don't treat your stepchildren like stepchildren.

For a healthy marriage and healthy children, let your children sleep in their own bed – not yours.

Don't allow your children to play you against each other.

Stepchildren are your children by covenant. Bless your spouse, do something loving for your stepchildren even the difficult ones.

A spouse who is connected more emotionally to the children is an unhealthy one.

Stepfamilies need to blend as one. Don't be separate in dealing with your children.

Jesus was Joseph's stepson but no one called him that or treated him as such. He was referred to as the son of Joseph.

COMMITMENT

> *Therefore shall a man leave his father and mother and shall cleave to his wife and they shall be one flesh. Genesis 2:24 KJV*

It's funny how we are so committed to our children. They can do some crazy stuff, but nothing they do can cause us to give up on them. We need to be the same way about our spouses.

Marriage is not forever...but it is for a lifetime.

Commitment is a constant, not a variable.

Never give up, no matter what tough stuff is thrown in your path.

If your marriage is at risk, seek help. Sometimes you are too broken to hold it together alone.

The ability to keep holding on is what gets you to a lifetime.

Love never fails or gives up or leaves.

You can't get to a lifetime without fully committing to your spouse.

Anybody can get married, but it takes real strength to stay married.

Esteem your spouse more than work and ministry, because the truth is everything vies to get between married lovers.

Commitment is shown in the tough times. Its shown when you want to give up but you don't.

Leaving doesn't make the problems go away. It multiplies them.

Covenant breakers are people who gave up on their promise.

The best thing about marriage is its permanent design.

Eliminating the option to give up, forces couples to work that much harder to make the marriage work.

Begin with the thought of being married for a lifetime and carry that thought to the end.

Marriage is the strength of our society. When we allow it to break down or be redefined, our society disintegrates.

What does it take to make a marriage last? A genuine relationship with God and a willingness to change.

COMMUNICATION

> *My dear brothers and sisters, take note of this: Everyone should be quick to listen, slow to speak and slow to become angry, James 1:19 NIV*

Improve your marriage: Give your spouse your COMPLETE attention when she/he is speaking. Zone in. Focus. Turn off your phone, television, ipad, and computer. Turn off all the distractions in your head.

Your problems won't just fade away. You really have to work on them

When conducting your husband-wife meetings, the two of you should come together to strategically attack the issues - not each other. You should not be pitted against each other. Remember you are teammates forever!

Listening involves hearing your spouse's heart and not just their words.

A wise spouse takes time to think before speaking.

Conflict in your relationship is NOT a sign of marital trouble. It is an opportunity to grow in your relationship by finding the right solution.

Is your home a sanctuary or a nest of negativity? You can have what you say.

Sometimes after we remove all the defensiveness, pride, and hurt, we will find that we were really saying the same thing.

Expectations that are not communicated will most likely be unrealized expectations resulting in disappointment.

Nagging comes from those who think they can change another with their steady pounding of negative words. However the nagged learn how to effectively tune the nagger out. Nagging becomes like background noise.

Communicate even that which you think is OBVIOUS - because it isn't always.

Give your spouse your full attention when he/she is speaking. A team player doesn't zone out.

When you are offended by your spouse, do not hold it in and simmer. Talk it out and forgive.

In all your getting, get an understanding. (Prov 4:7) You can't afford to shut down or withdraw. Keep talking until you reach an understanding. Your marriage depends on it.

The biggest obstacle to effective communication is when one spouse does not listen to the other. It's not enough to present your case.

Sometimes a couple is trying to say the same thing but using different words. Slow down, diffuse the emotion and listen to your spouse. You may be closer to a resolution than you think.

Don't push your spouse's buttons. The result can be harmful to your relationship.

The silent treatment is a poor way to treat your spouse. While you are silent, the enemy is speaking to the both of you.

Husbands and wives communicate differently. The smart marriage does well to remember this.

Don't take every biting word to heart. You don't always mean what you say in the heat of the moment and neither does your spouse.

The silent treatment is a manipulative and hurtful weapon. It should only be used against an enemy. NEVER in a marriage.

If you want a harsh spouse, feed them harsh words. If you want a sweet spouse, feed them sweet words.

Carefully choose each and every word you speak to your spouse and children. Speak life.

For better problem solving, listen to your spouse's words. Don't prepare what you will say next.

DATE NIGHT

> *May your fountain be blessed, and may you rejoice in the wife of your youth. Proverbs 5:18 NIV*

Real lovers never stop dating.

Date night is a simple thing that couples can do to strengthen their marriages. Don't ignore the simple things.

The best marriages make dating a necessary part of what they do to keep love alive.

Be creative with your date nights. Don't get locked into dinner and a movie. Do something exciting and different.

Don't stop the romance. Whatever it took to capture your spouse's heart, it will take to keep it.

Date night is a gift that you give to your marriage.

Don't skip your date nights. An appointment with your spouse is just as important as any other. Take time to invest in your marriage.

Invite fun into your relationship every week by dating each other.

A healthy relationship is dependent on the time we are willing to sow into it. Give your spouse at least one day out of seven.

If you find it difficult finding a babysitter for date nights, identify a couple with the same issue and trade babysitting – alternate weeks.

Carving out time for your spouse gives your spouse something to look forward to each week.

It is healthy for couples to getaway periodically to revive and refresh the marriage.

The best date nights are the ones in which we spend the most imagination not the most money.

Dating your spouse doesn't have to be at night. The most important thing is that you are spending time together.

Don't just go through the motions of having a date night. Seek to connect with your spouse.

DIVORCE

> *The man who hates and **divorces** his wife," says the Lord, the God of Israel, "does violence to the one he should protect," says the Lord Almighty. So be on your guard, and do not be unfaithful.*
> *Malachi 2:16 NIV*

A marriage doesn't just break down. Somewhere along the line, the spouses stopped working on it and caring for it.

Marriage is not for quitters.

No marriage is TOO HARD for God. ...If only we would just give it to Him

Marriage is an idol in our culture. We divorce in pursuit of the "perfect" marriage. (It's the one we see in the movies). We search for someone to complete us or to make us happy. And we will NEVER find it. Real marriage is between two imperfect people who have lots of challenges but find their fulfillment in Christ.

Divorce is an assault against God's power and an insult on his character. Divorce says God couldn't fix it.

Divorce has never been in God's plan. He hates divorce. We should too.

Marriage is ministry. If you give up on your spouse, you will give up on those who have the same hang-ups. So thankful that God does NOT give up on us.

You cannot despise your spouse but love God. It's just not possible.

Declare your house a divorce-free zone. Do not speak the "d" word as a threat. Do not even entertain thoughts of something that God says He hates.

Our culture has made marriage an idol. We esteem it as the panacea for all our ills. Because we buy into the Hollywood hype, when it doesn't go well we drop out and into another one – chasing after the relationship high.

The biggest trick the enemy uses against couples struggling in marriage is - that once you have lost love, there is no way to get it back. If you are willing, God is able.

In order to give up on your marriage, you must first give up on God (and His miracle working power).

Don't threaten each other with the "d" word in the heat of an argument. It's just not productive. Make your home a divorce-free zone

FORGIVENESS

> *Be kind and compassionate to one another, forgiving each other, just as in Christ God forgave you. Ephesians 4:32 NIV*

Forgiveness is a choice - not an emotion. You can choose it before you "feel" it.

There is no way around it. We MUST forgive if we are going to be married for a lifetime.

Forgive like it's your last day on earth.

"I'm sorry" are two powerful words that when spoken with sincerity can shift the atmosphere of your marriage. Try them.

If God forgives your spouse, why can't you?
You cannot get to a lifetime of love without forgiveness. #don'tleavehomewithoutit

Two of the most underused words in marriages – I'm sorry. Sometimes, that's all it takes.

You can't afford unforgiveness in your marriage. The price is too high.

Don't keep count on who apologizes first. Just do it for Christ's sake.

I'm Sorry - two very important words that help a marriage last for a lifetime.

It is counterproductive to pull an offense out of a past closet to strengthen a present argument.

In order to forgive your spouse means you cannot keep meditating on the offense or talking about it. You act as if it NEVER happened. Isn't that how God does us?

Let's right all those strained relationships. If you owe an apology -give it. If someone owes you an apology, forgive them.

Sometimes we mistakenly think that if we forgive an offense, the spouse will repeat it (as if unforgiveness is a cure for sin and offense). Forgiveness cleans the hurt out. Unforgiveness keeps it there.

It's funny how we can easily justify why we should be forgiven. But we struggle with forgiving someone else.

Forgive to live.

GOD-CENTERED

> *Though one may be overpowered, two can defend themselves A cord of three strands is not quickly broken. Ecclesiastes 4:12 NIV*

Let's treat marriage as if it sprung from the heart of God. He really does know what He's doing.

A 3-fold cord is not easily broken. Marriage works when we keep it in the hands of the One who created it.

"You complete me." It sounds so romantic. But it is really contrary to who Christ is in us. Our spouses do not complete us. If our spouse could complete us where is our need for a Savior?

Marriage is not a curse. It's an amazing blessing when you put God first.

The Bible is the best marriage manual ever written. All we have to do it is apply it.

Marriage is God's idea. In order to have success, we must follow his plan.

In order to have "Holy Matrimony", you must keep the Holy One at the core of your matrimony.

Do not idolize your marriage or your spouse. Worship God only.

In order to win it, God must be in it.

Connect with other healthy married couples. It's good for your relationship. Iron sharpens iron.

The closer we are to God, the closer we are to one another.

Praying for your spouse is a good starting place. However the strongest marriages pray with their spouse.

Smart marriages do marriage by the book. They follow the plans of the Designer.

Pray in faith for your marriage. Believe God to heal, strengthen or restore your marriage.

He is God of the impossible. Nothing and no one is out of his reach.

HONESTY

> *An **honest** answer is like a kiss on the lips.*
> *Proverbs 24:26 NIV*

Sometimes spouses are not honest with each other for fear of hurt feelings. Decide to speak the truth in love to your spouse and work through the negative feelings. You will have a healthier marriage.

When you lie to your spouse, you are also lying to yourself.

Deceit destroys a marriage from the inside out.

Be open and honest with your spouse, even when it hurts.

If you lie to your mate just one time, he/she can never know when you are telling the truth.

You have to give your spouse an opportunity to hear the truth. Don't prejudge whether or not they can handle it. Either way, you don't have the right to withhold it from them.

Telling your spouse nothing is wrong when you are offended is dishonest and unfair behavior.

Don't support your spouse when he/she is choosing to sin. Challenge him/her to righteousness. Remember Ananias and Sapphira.

Hiding passwords and purchases are the fruit of a dishonest person.

No one should hold more knowledge than your spouse about what's going on in your life.

Be naked and vulnerable. Share your weaknesses/failures with your spouse.

Secrets ultimately harm a marriage.

Fear of rejection will make you vulnerable to deceit.

Do not cover your failures from your spouse. Intimacy is built in sharing the successes and the failures.

Integrity is where trust comes from.

God has changed many dishonest hearts. No one is without hope.

Pray for a dishonest spouse.

HONOR

> *Be devoted to one another in love, honor one another above yourselves. Romans 12:10 NIV*

Every wife should feel spoiled by her husband and every husband should feel spoiled by his wife.

A sensitive spouse is a wise spouse. Do NOT make jokes at your spouse's expense.

Care about the things that are important to your spouse.

You should be willing to change some things in your life just because the love of your life asks you.

Spouses should not curse at each other. It's disrespectful to yourself, your spouse, and to your God.

Tomorrow is promised to none of us. Don't take your spouse for granted. Enjoy him/her while there is time.

Don't reject your spouse's calls or ignore his/her texts.

Your spouse should be your first priority after God.

Making jokes at your spouse's expense undermines and damages the relationship.

You strengthen your marriage when you refuse to allow family members and friends to disrespect your spouse.

Your best friend should be your spouse. Never should it be someone of the opposite gender. Even if he/she was your friend before you met your spouse. Spouse is automatically moved to first position.

Support your spouse in the area where you have been the least supportive, and watch your marriage grow.

Married couples whenever you are flying solo, handling business, or running errands, conduct yourself as if your spouse is present.

Don't treat your spouse like a child. Be respectful.

Give your spouse your attention. Cut off the phone, ipad, ipod, television, computer, video games, etc. Your spouse deserves your undivided attention.

IN-LAWS

> *Honor thy father and thy mother that thy days may be long upon the land which the Lord thy God giveth thee. Exodus 20:12 KJV*

Your in-laws are your parents by law... and by love.

It would do a mother-in-law well to remember she used to be a daughter-in-law and the daughter-in-well to know that one day she may be a mother-in-law.

If you want a better in-law relationship, be a better in-law.

Wisdom says do not share the struggles in your marriage with your family. When you and spouse have worked it out and have forgiven and forgotten, your family will still remember and most often they will be a little less forgiving.

Sometimes parents need help in letting go of their adult children; it is the responsibility of the newlywed couple to help them draw clear boundaries.

Forgive your in-laws. Love them like they are your own family.

When there is an issue, a spouse should confront his/her own parent.

Often a daughter in law complains that her mother in law doesn't treat her like a daughter, but the daughter in law should make sure that she is treating her mom in law like a mom.

There is NEVER a good reason to disrespect your in-laws.

Sowing seeds of love and respect into your spouse's family will cause you to reap a harvest in your marriage.

Every family has set traditions and ways of operating; it is unwise for a newlywed to come in thinking that she is going to "change" the family dynamic.

Leaving your parents to cleave to your spouse only speaks to priority. It doesn't mean ignore or abandon your relationship with them.

The in-law relationship can be difficult to navigate. Be patient, kind, and forgiving as this new relationship emerges.

Pray for your spouse's family as if they were your own...because they are.

Don't allow your parents or siblings to speak negatively about your spouse in or out of your presence.

Respect your parents but don't allow their opinions to have more weight in your marriage than your spouse's.

Everyone must adjust when a couple gets married; allow time for the adjustment, pray for the adjustment. Be patient but make sure the boundaries are clear.

LOVE

> *Love must be sincere. Romans 12:9 NIV*

True love is not based upon merit. We should not withhold our love because someone doesn't act like we think they should. We love them because they need us to.

Love your spouse completely. Don't hold back. Tomorrow is promised to none of us.

In our vows, we claim to love for better or for worse. So hang in there when the worse shows up.

The most basic component of love is forgiveness.

Love is an action word. Make sure you love in deed and not in word only.

You show God you love Him by loving on your spouse.

Love is so much more than a feeling. It would do married couples well to remember that: love even when you don't feel like it.

You can't fall out of love. Real love has no ending.

God's love for us is permanent. We ought to have that same type of love for our spouse.

Love never fails...in trials, sickness, job loss, pain, trouble communicating, financial distress, rebellious children, meddling in-laws, discouragement, ministry, business success, business failure, etc.

While there is much more to love than saying it, it still needs to be said.

The best part of love is in its expression. Demonstrate love to your spouse.

Love always looks for the good in the relationship.

Real love waits on his/her spouse to change.

Love is kind. Watch how you treat your spouse.

Love sees the best part of their spouse when no one else can.

Married persons should come into the marriage expecting to serve their spouse.

LOYALTY

> Many claim to have unfailing love, but a faithful person who can find? Proverbs 12:6 NIV

Loyalty is an attribute of a strong marriage. It requires that you do not tear your spouse down or expose his/her faults to others.

It is disloyal to share your complaints, criticisms, and annoyances about your spouse with your friends and family members.

Your marriage is your first ministry.

The two stand united and always present a united front.

A faithful wife's ear can only hear that which is uplifting to her spouse.

Your spouse comes before all your speaking engagements, congregants, and ministerial duties.

A healthy marriage is strong on loyalty. Spouses defend one another, refuse to let others trample on their relationship, don't blast their issues on social media and never gossip about the other.

Beware of "friends" who speak negatively about your spouse (especially when you are upset with your spouse).

A loyal spouse doesn't throw his/her spouse under the bus. Love covers.

Loyalty is not an option but a requirement in a strong thriving marriage.

The loyal spouse will not let his/her eyes wander. His/Her eyes stay where their promise is.

Do not discredit your spouse when you two are in a disagreement. It is the unwise spouse who paints their spouse as the villain to get others to agree with him/her.

A loyal spouse hurts when his/her mate hurts.

A faithful wife doesn't go behind her husband's back to manipulate to get her way.

Loyalty upholds and enforces what a spouse has spoken.

When you took your vows, it was just the two of you before the minister. Don't let others define your relationship.

MONEY

> *Wisdom is a shelter as money is a shelter. But the advantage of knowledge is this wisdom preserves those who have it. Ecclesiastes 7:12*

Smart marriages maintain financial integrity. They do not hide purchases, money, or credit cards.

Great advice for married couples : Live BENEATH your means. Your total expenses should be significantly lower than your total income. If not, you are headed for financial disaster. Make the necessary adjustments today!!!

It's not a good strategy for your marriage to have a secret stash. While it may seem prudent for the moment, it is really counterproductive for the long run.

Stop blowing the budget and then complaining about not having enough money.

Avoid a fiscal cliff in your house. Get on one accord with spending and saving. It's the road to prosperity.

Think long and hard before borrowing money; for it is true that the borrower is servant to the lender.

Couples should operate from 1 money pot. Separating your bank accounts and splitting the bills does not allow you to get the best advantage in your finances.

There is an automatic blessing when you are one in your finances.

Don't let the pressure from friends and relatives push you outside of your financial season. If it's a time to save, then save. Others may be in a different season or just plain reckless. Don't get caught up in keeping up with the proverbial "Joneses".

It's easier for each spouse to stick to the budget if both are allotted pocket money (to spend on incidentals).

STOP unnecessary spending. Get a spending plan and stick to it. 'Money Problems' is one of the top reasons couple's divorce.

Being in a marriage is to be a part of a team. Consult your team before making large purchases, opening new accounts, loaning money.

Pray over your income and expenses. Then follow God's instruction.

Take some stress off of your relationship by making it a priority to live debt-free.

Emergencies will come; so be sure to have an emergency savings account to meet them when they show up.

Money is not evil. It's the way that we respond to money that determines whether evil is present.

The secret to financial stability is to live BENEATH your means.

Every couple should have savings, both short term and long term.

Savings and insurance build a hedge around your lifestyle. They keep you from financial devastation.

Beware: Borrowing money from family and friends can sometimes come with invisible strings attached.

It is prudent for both spouses to know the state of the finances.

ONENESS

> *That is why a man leaves his father and mother and is united to his wife and they become one flesh. Genesis 2:24 NIV*

In order to become one, you MUST be willing to change. Change involves forgiving, adjusting, learning and growing. Otherwise you get stuck in your ways and the marriage goes sour.

There is fun-ness in oneness.

You may not always agree, but always be one.

Two are better than one. Utilize the power of your team. You will be much more successful.

You do NOT become one the day you say, "I Do". Marriage is the process of becoming one. It is about giving and receiving. It's letting go of the single "you" and embracing the new you who is a part of the team.

In order to become one, you must buy into the concept of team.

Choose what's best for the marriage, not the individual.

Harness the strength of your team. If your spouse is gifted in the area of finances, he or she should be the one handling the finances. Utilize each other's gifts to strengthen your team.

Do not loan money to your parents, siblings, other family or friends when your spouse does not agree.

A healthy marriage is when both spouses understand that his/her spouse is not the enemy." Then the two team together against the real enemy of their union – Satan.

Be on the same side. Never let anyone divide you.

Your differences strengthen your team.

Pray together, it brings you closer.

If you both agree with God, you will agree with one another.

The more you two agree with the word, the more you will become one.

There is real strength in unity.

Let no one and no issue come between you.

SELFISHNESS

> *Let each of you look not only to your own interests but also to the interests of others.*
> *Philippians 2:4 ESV*

We must continually work on our love relationship with the Lord. It is only by loving Him that we can properly love our spouses.

The more we die, the more our marriages live.

Selfishness does not make a strong marriage. It opposes the two becoming one.

Your flesh negatively impacts your marriage. Kill it.

Don't try to change your spouse. It's an impossible task. Try something a little easier - changing yourself.

You cannot hold on to your marriage and act like a married bachelor or married bachelorette. A strong marriage requires that you commit to your team.

Remember, you work on your marriage by working on yourself.

You should not be same person you were on the day you married. You should grow and be stretched into someone better

It is easy to see our spouse's faults. But the word encourages us to do something a little more challenging - see our own faults and correct them. Then we can lovingly help our spouse. (motes and beams)

If your marriage is in a bad place, don't dump all the responsibility on your spouse. Begin change by taking responsibility for your part

Marriage is ministry. It's a life of serving and putting your spouse's needs above your own.

If we are growing as individuals (by afflicting our flesh), we will see the results in a growing marriage.

It's not all about you and your feelings. Consider others more than yourself.

When accessing all the wrong in your marriage, make sure you take a good look in the mirror first.

Independence will kill a union. Interdependence works best in marriage.

SEX

> *The husband should fulfill his marital duty to his wife, and likewise the wife to her husband. The wife does not have authority over her own body but yields it to her husband. In the same way, the husband does not have authority over his own body but yields it to his wife. Corinthians 7:3-4 NIV*

Sex was never meant to be used as a weapon. Withholding sex from your spouse to punish him/her is ungodly and manipulative.

Invite God into your bedroom. Begin your experience with prayer and watch your love life transform.

Don't take your physical relationship for granted. Thank your spouse for making love to you.

Married sex is the best sex.

Sex is a great stress reliever.

Take your time: explore and enjoy each other's bodies.

Make love to her heart before her body.

Have sex as often as possible. Quantity will change with the seasons of your life.

Compliment your spouse in bed. It makes your physical relationship that much better.

Connect emotionally and spiritually and the fireworks will come.

Increase your physical intimacy for just $30 bucks: add a lock to your bedroom door.

Heighten your sexual experience: involve all 5 senses in the bedroom.

Sexual images (from movies, books, etc) block intimacy. Let your images be of each other.

Marital relations create a godly soul tie.

Don't use sex as a substitute for communication.

Your sex life is private; keep it between the two of you.

Seek to pleasure your spouse and you both benefit.

SUBMISSION

> *Submit to one another out of reverence for Christ. Ephesians 5:21 NIV*

Submission is not how you respond when you agree. It's how you respond when you disagree.

When the husband lets the wife take his decision-making responsibilities, he feels off the hook but he resents it. Resentment is the silent killer of marriages.

Submission cannot be demanded. It must be granted. A wife that feels loved will offer it freely.

Ladies, true submission is when you follow your husband's heart, not just his words.

You don't always have to be right in your marriage. Stop lecturing your mate, or having to have the last word. Very few people want to be around a know-it-all. Strong communication requires that we admit when we err and we study to be quiet.

Control breeds rebellion.

Allow your husband the freedom to follow what He believes God is saying.

Wives are not to take control of her husband's spiritual leadership. Wait on him.

The call to submission is not just to wives but to husbands as well.

Our first submission is due to God.

The time to submit is when you don't agree.

Submission is never the problem, rebellion is.

If a husband is passive, the wife should not take his place as leader of the home. Leave his space available for him when he steps up.

A leader does not have to run every decision he makes by those he leads.

You can always go over your husband's head by going down on your knees. Prayer will change his heart.

A healthy marriage is when Christ is at the head, a husband leads and the wife follows.

If we think submission is out of style or old fashioned, we lose the heart of what makes marriages work.

Prayer gives us the power to submit.

TRUST

> *Now it is required that those who have been given a trust must prove faithful.*
> *I Corinthians 4:2 NIV*

Jealousy is unattractive. It is a sign that the relationship is unhealthy.

It takes just a few seconds to destroy trust; but it can take several years to rebuild.

Think hard and long before making decisions that could cost you more than you're willing to lose.

Share your passwords with each other. Show that you trust and are trustworthy.

Keep a safe distance with co-workers and others with whom you spend lots of time. Conduct yourself as if your spouse is present.

It takes courage to reach intimacy in marriage. Be vulnerable with your spouse.

Trust is a gift from your spouse. Handle it carefully. If you break it, it is much more difficult to get your spouse to give it to you again.

When your spouse is open and honest with you, don't use it against him/her.

Locking your phone is not about whether your spouse is trustworthy but whether you are.

Never accuse your spouse even if it seems that you are right. Ask, don't assume.

You can only trust to the level of your intimacy.

Dress in a way that honors your spouse.

Trust can be built through adversity.

Don't fight in public or in public view (social media, etc.). Trust is damaged in the open.

When you have broken trust, don't expect your spouse to just get over it. You must be patient and understanding.

Don't withhold trust. Even if it's been broken, work at restoring it.

Take care to avoid potentially dangerous situations with the opposite sex.

Wisdom Bites for the Whole Marriage

WISDOM FOR WIVES

Wise wives speak life giving words about their husbands and avoid the temptation to complain.

Husbands do not "just" know what you need every time you need it. They do not think like women. If you want or need something, ladies, don't sit there pouting. Speak up. It makes married life a whole lot easier.

She does him good and not harm all the days of his life Proverbs 31

A wife wants her husband to share his heart with her. But a husband has to be able to trust his wife with his heart. Ladies, don't use what he shares against him.

Don't wait for and expect your spouse to fail. Remind him/her of important dates (birthdays, anniversaries, etc). You will both feel better for it.

If you ask your husband a question, brace yourself for an answer you may not want to hear. Don't lash out at him for answering with truth, lest you train him to tell you only what you want to hear.

Don't say things to your husband that you wouldn't want him to say to you.

Crying can be a way of manipulating your spouse for control.

Trust the God in him.

You really do have control over your emotions. Submit them to the spirit of God.

Don't compare your spouse with someone else. You didn't marry someone else.

If he doesn't do what you expect, it doesn't mean he doesn't love you.

Don't neglect your husband. Give him the attention and affection he longs for.

Men and women think differently. Don't expect him to act and/or think like a woman.

Wives, please don't expect your husbands to read your mind. And then when you don't get what you were expecting, you get upset. Be proactive. Tell your husband what you would like for Valentine's Day...and any day. He's not going to know unless you tell him. Leave the romantic fantasy to Hollywood.

You can't say that you have a bad marriage because one area is out of order. Don't make a whole judgment on the part.

Be his dream wife.

Be the type of wife you would want your son to marry and your daughter to emulate.

Let him be free to be himself.

Nagging him will not change him. It only frustrates you.

PMS is not a free pass to act out. A godly woman walks in God's love.

There is freedom in submission.

God can make him better than you can. Trust God with your spouse.

WISDOM FOR HUSBANDS

Tell your wife everyday that you love her.

Men must provide for their families, protect them and lead them as the priest of his home.

Treat your wife like she really is your "good thing".

Remember the things that are important to her.

Lead her even when she doesn't want to follow.

Submission is not "just" for wives. It is for all believers.

If you agree to complete a project or chore, do it. It makes for a peaceful home.

Listen to your wife. God will use her to speak to you.

If you offend your wife, don't expect her to just get over "it". She is not male. Females have to process their emotions in order to let it go. Listen to her with an understanding heart.

Don't be content with the norm. Actively chase after your wife daily.

Remember your favor is connected to the way your treat your wife.

Don't neglect your wife. Give her the attention and affection she longs for.

A wife's love is a gift, and a husband is but the steward of it.

The wise husband includes his wife in working the budget. It is important for both spouses to know the state of the finances.

Ask God to lead you as you lead your home.

Humility will take you a lot further than your pride.

A man's love beautifies his wife.

Be man enough to ask for forgiveness.

Giving cannot compensate for a lack of love; give her you, not just things.

Be the type of husband you would want your daughter to choose and your son to emulate.

Believe that you have the best wife in the world, and then act accordingly.

Be her dream husband.

Kiss her for no reason at all.

Talk to your wife, not at her.

Share your dreams, your heart, and your life with your wife.

Be willing to help with the chores. Team work is the best work.

Don't get lazy in your marriage. Seek to win her heart again and again through romance.

Flirt with your wife, not another woman.

BUILDING A HEALTHY RELATIONSHIP

In order for the tools to work in your marriage, you have to use them.

Your best friend ought not be someone of the opposite gender. Work on making your spouse your best friend.

The way you treat your spouse is the way he/she will respond.

A marriage left to itself will disintegrate. Our relationships must be intentional. Let's do them in and on purpose.

Don't smother your spouse. Give each other space in your relationship. Time out with the girls or with the guys will do wonders for your marriage.

Invest in your marriage: Get involved in as much marriage ministry as you can. You will reap great returns.

We don't always do what we know to do to improve our marriages. We usually pick the easiest things on the list. Today pick a tough one and take your marriage to the next level.

To be a happy spouse, you must think happy thoughts. Arrest those negative thoughts about your spouse and kick them out of your happy space.

If we all agree that the Bible is the best marriage manual, then we should make a commitment to follow the instructions.

Celebrate every good thing about your relationship.

Don't settle for a mediocre marriage. Turn it up.

Marriage is not as easy as it looks. It takes God's love, commitment, and loads of forgiveness.

Strengthen your marriage. Read a book, attend a conference/workshop, listen to a cd, get counseling. Be committed for a lifetime.

The best way to get a spouse to change his/her behavior is with prayer, loving kindness and patience.

Don't compare your spouse to someone else. You didn't marry someone else. Celebrate your spouse's strengths.

No matter how good you believe your marriage is, keep looking to improve it - there is always room.

Marriage does come with instructions - (The Word). We just need to follow them.

Your friends don't have a free pass to speak against your spouse, no matter how long the relationship.

Dream together and then put it in a book. (Create a dream book.)

Don't compare your marriage to someone else's. Each relationship has different ingredients and starting points. We may not grow at the same pace, but we can all finish well.

HOPE FOR HURTING MARRIAGES

When your marriage hits a rough patch, don't just throw in the towel. This is the time to work it out.

'For better and for worse'...reminds us to stay the course in the worst moments.

Don't define your marriage by one incident.

Many people who divorce regret that they didn't fight harder and longer.

Speak life to your marriage, no matter how dead it feels.

A good, strong marriage is not out of reach. There just aren't enough people reaching for it.

If you want your marriage to be different, then you cannot follow the same old patterns.

Do-it-yourself marriage counseling does not work. Seek help when you are hurting.

In order to heal, you will have to make a decision to let go of your anger.

Ask God for help. He will help if you want him to.

When there is a problem in the marriage, look for a solution. Don't look to be right.

Don't let your relationship go down without a good fight.

You married your spouse because God dropped the idea of marriage into the earth. And you decided to agree with Him. It's all for His glory.

If you are afraid to talk to your spouse about your concerns (because he/she may explode), this is a sign that the relationship may be unhealthy. Seek counseling immediately

Your spouse cannot make you happy or unhappy. You must take responsibility for your own emotions.

Many marriages have hit rough seasons and have been able to recover.

In spite of what you have seen in media, there is nothing easy about making a marriage work.

The longest lasting marriages have had more challenges, but they keep on pressing.

Focus on what's good about your marriage and build from there.

Sometimes marriages are faced with the most difficult challenges: pornography, adultery, domestic violence, addictions. But know this - whatever you may face, God is able to heal and deliver. Don't give up. Seek help.

If your marriage is headed down the wrong path, be proactive. Turn it around.

An apology is best demonstrated.

If you meditate on the good that your spouse has done instead of the bad, you will feel better and act better toward him/her. This makes your marriage smile

No matter how hard it seems at the moment, it is ALWAYS best to follow God and His plan.

Marriage makes us better.

Love covers.

"I do" is not a life sentence. It's a pledge to love for life.

Expect change to come. Don't expect failure.

Every marriage hits a hard spot.

About Oscar & Crystal Jones

Oscar & Crystal Jones have been celebrating their covenant love affair for over 32 years. They have 7 children (which include 1 daughter-in-law and 1 son-in-law). They are also the happy grandparents of 6.

Oscar & Crystal are both teachers by trade. They have both taught in the private and public sectors. Both have left the education system for full-time ministry.

Pastors Oscar & Crystal have a unique Aquila and Priscilla team ministry. They lavishly love the Lord and one another. God has coupled this into a special anointing and gifted them to be able to minister from the pulpit as one voice.

They are founders of **Marriage for a Lifetime Ministries** in Atlanta, GA, **Greater Works Family Ministries** in Detroit, MI, and **Agape International Association of Churches and Para-churches**, The two have been featured guests on several radio and television broadcasts. They host a monthly teleconference where they discuss issues relevant to marriage and the family. They also put on Couples Cafes where they come in costumes and armed with props to teach on different marriage topics.

The Joneses celebrate all things marriage.

The couple sponsor The **Tending The Bride Marriage Retreat** for senior pastors and their spouses. The couple has authored several books together and apart. They aspire to leave a legacy of hope and healing to the body of Christ.

Marriage For A Lifetime Ministries

www.marriage4alifetime.org
email: jones@marriage4alifetime.org
Facebook: Marriage For A Lifetime Ministries
Twitter: Marriage4Life

Books By The Authors

A Woman's Place: Leading Ladies Speak Compiled by Crystal Jones & Joceline Bronson

Extreme Money Makeover by Oscar & Crystal Jones

LeaderShift 3.0 by Oscar & Crystal Jones

Naked Sex (For Married Couples Only) by Oscar & Crystal Jones

No Longer A Dream: Step by Step Guide to Writing Your First Book
-by Crystal Jones

Not Without My Daughters: The Beginner's Guide to Mentoring and Being Mentored by Crystal Jones

Restore The Roar by Oscar Jones

Ring Talks by Oscar & Crystal Jones
The Newlywed Handbook by Oscar & Crystal Jones

The S Word: What Submission Is Not by Crystal Jones

When The Vow Breaks by Oscar & Crystal Jones

www.ingramcontent.com/pod-product-compliance
Lightning Source LLC
Chambersburg PA
CBHW061500040426
42450CB00008B/1429